Cardinal Basil Hume

Also 'In My Own Words':

Leo Tolstoy

Mother Teresa

Pope John XXIII

Pope John Paul II

Cardinal Basil Hume

In My Own Words

Compiled and edited by
TERESA DE BERTODANO

Hodder & Stoughton
LONDON   SYDNEY   AUCKLAND

British Library Cataloguing in Publication Data
A record for this book is available from the British Library

ISBN 0 340 75610 1

Typeset in Adobe Goudy Old Style by
Strathmore Publishing Services, London N7

Printed and bound in Great Britain by
Clays Ltd, St Ives plc

Hodder and Stoughton Ltd
A Division of Hodder Headline PLC
338 Euston Road
London NW1 3BH

If we were to ask what a bishop
should be as we enter the third millennium
he would be just such a person as Basil Hume.

CARLO MARIA MARTINI
CARDINAL ARCHBISHOP OF MILAN

CONTENTS

ACKNOWLEDGMENTS

Miss Heather Craufurd gathered together many of Cardinal Hume's writings and prepared them for publication. This book draws substantially upon her work.

The book could not have been completed without the valued assistance of Sally McAllister and Colette Young. Dom Benedict Webb, Sub-Prior of Ampleforth, has been a tower of strength. I am grateful to my brother Martin de Bertodano, to Jeanne Bisgood, to the Tyburn community and to Dr Thérèse Vanier. Also to Judith Longman of Hodder and Stoughton for inviting me to make this compilation with the agreement of Cardinal Hume's literary executors, Mr Charles Wookey and Fr Liam Kelly. I am grateful to them for allowing me access to unpublished material and to Fr Gerald O'Collins sj for kindly reading the manuscript. I am grateful to Fr Vladimir Felzmann for permission to reproduce an extract from *Lourdes and its Values*, and to Julie Hatherall of Hodder and Stoughton.

The following publications by Cardinal Hume have been drawn upon:

Ampleforth Journal.
Searching for God, Hodder and Stoughton, 1977 and
     1990.
In Praise of Benedict, Ampleforth Abbey Press, 1981.
To Be a Pilgrim, St Paul Publications, 1984.
Towards a Civilisation of Love, Hodder and Stoughton,
     1988.
Light in the Lord, St Paul Publications, 1991.
Lourdes and its Values, privately published, 1991.
Remaking Europe, SPCK, 1994.
Footprints of the Northern Saints, DLT, 1996.
The Mystery of Love, Hodder and Stoughton, 1996.
Basil in Blunderland, DLT, 1997.
The Mystery of the Cross, DLT, 1998.
Millennium Lenten Meditations, Westminster Cathedral,
     1999.
The Mystery of the Incarnation, DLT, 1999.

Other material is taken from unpublished talks and sermons. Some of the material accredited to a single published source has appeared in an identical or similar form in several publications. Where it has not been possible to identify a published source, accreditation is given to its unpublished archive.

$\mathcal{I}$NTRODUCTION

[Basil Hume] kept our secrets, consulted us generously and often overcame the universal temptation to believe that one can do everything better oneself and cannot find the time to teach others to do it.[1]

BARNABAS SANDEMAN OSB

The secret of the love and devotion inspired by this most unassuming of men perhaps lies in Dom Barnabas' gentle qualification 'Hume *often* overcame ...' Similarly, Bishop John Crowley, in the homily at Cardinal Hume's funeral, described him as being *almost* entirely at peace during his final days.

George Basil Hume knew what it was to try and to fail – and to keep battling on. As a schoolmaster he would have been quick to tell his boys 'if at first you

don't succeed try to hide your astonishment!' In an
early interview with a tabloid newspaper he revealed
that he believed himself to have been 'over assessed'
and was thinking of starting 'a society for the de-
mythologising of Hume'.

George Hume was born in Newcastle on 2 March
1923, the elder son of a family of three girls and two
boys. Sir William Hume was a consultant physician
and Professor of Medicine at Durham University. His
wife was a French Roman Catholic and Sir William
was content that she should bring up the family in her
own religious tradition. In this she seems to have been
conspicuously successful. It is said that upon occasion
Lady Hume was accused of 'making mixed marriages
look too easy'.

Newcastle during the thirties had its grim side.
While the Humes lived comfortably they were aware
that others were less fortunate. A Dominican priest
took George to visit the poorer parts of Tyneside
which made a profound impression. Early stirrings
of a religious vocation inclined him towards the
Dominicans but his teenage years at school at Ampleforth ensured that he would eventually opt to join the
Benedictine monastery in 1941 as 'Brother Basil'.

Ampleforth during the Second World War provided
a strict regime for novices under the jurisdiction of

Abbot Herbert Byrne. From 1944 to 1947 Basil read history at Oxford and during this period took solemn vows as a Benedictine monk, thus committing himself for life to the Ampleforth community. From 1947 to 1951 he studied theology in Switzerland at Fribourg University, returning to the monastery to be ordained priest on 23 July 1950.

In 1951 Hume became an assistant priest in Ampleforth village and began teaching theology to the younger monks as well as modern languages and history in the school. As a housemaster he was also responsible for the care of more than sixty boys and from 1951 to 1963 coached the Rugby XV – always maintaining his own lifelong commitment to the foot-balling fortunes of his beloved Newcastle United.

In 1963 this busy life moved into a higher gear when Hume's community elected him Abbot. Hume was a reluctant candidate. Immediately after the election the former Abbot announced that the first problem facing Abbot Hume was his predecessor. What was he going to do with Abbot Byrne?

'What would you like to do, Father?' enquired the new Abbot.

'I am waiting to be told. I have been telling other people what to do for twenty-four years!' Hume was eventually able to establish that Abbot Byrne would like to work in Leyland outside Liverpool, one of the parishes served by the Ampleforth community.

Hume's abbacy brought a wide range of ecumenical contacts which were to serve him well in later years. The sixties were not an easy period in monasteries and Abbot Hume bore the brunt of the changes brought about by the Second Vatican Council. He was influential within the English Benedictine Congregation but was otherwise little known beyond the north of England.

In 1975, on the death of Cardinal Heenan, this 'outsider' nevertheless found his name bandied about among those of candidates for successor to the See of Westminster. Hume was perhaps entertained by this new-found popularity. He did not appear to take his candidacy seriously. In a subsequent interview with a tabloid newspaper he said of his nomination, 'A bit of vanity made me ring up my mother to tell her my name was in the newspaper. She laughed! I was a bit hurt.' Hume's family seems to have been a constant and beloved influence in his life. The implication has been that they were as surprised as anyone by his appointment to Westminster.

The spirit in which the new Archbishop intended to fulfil his role was perhaps revealed at his installation in Westminster Cathedral on 25 March 1976, when he adapted St Augustine: 'I am a bishop for you. I am a Christian like you.' On the evening of that same day the new Archbishop and the Ampleforth community responded to the invitation of the Dean and Chapter of Westminster Abbey to sing solemn vespers in the Abbey. During his address Archbishop Hume foreshadowed future ecumenical relationships: 'We must discuss, we must have commissions, we must act together, but none of this will be of any avail unless we pray, and pray earnestly.'

Shortly after the installation Pope Paul VI announced that Archbishop Hume was to be created Cardinal and as Cardinal Archbishop of Westminster Hume became increasingly a 'national' figure. He was already a hardworking diocesan bishop.

Concern for Christian unity was a priority alongside a deep sense of identification with the disadvantaged. His visit to the Ethiopian famine victims in 1984 marked him for life.

Work for justice included an influential role in the liberation of the wrongly imprisoned 'Guildford Four' and the 'Maguire Seven'. The visit of Pope John Paul II to England, Scotland and Wales in 1982 was a triumph and alongside all this there were increasing commitments to the wider Church in Rome and elsewhere.

On Hume's visit to Rome as Archbishop-designate,

Pope Paul VI had told him 'You are a monk and must remain a monk.' There seems to have been little temptation to do otherwise. The things of the spirit remained a priority and Hume made no secret of his wish one day to resign from Westminster and return to his monastery 'or maybe have a little parish in the back of beyond'.

In a sense the twenty-three years at Westminster were 'the tip of the iceberg', in that the roots of his distinction lay in the previous forty years at his beloved Ampleforth. It was during the years as a teacher that he became convinced that 'every boy was in some way superior to me. He had some quality I did not possess or he could do something that I could not do – even if it was only mending a television set.' Hume remained convinced that every person he met was in some way superior to himself: an attitude which must have brought great healing in his contacts with those whom society frequently regards as outcast. Such contacts must also have been facilitated by the impression he gave of having 'had the corners knocked off' – an experience that is reasonably familiar to the successfully married but by no means always apparent among celibates.

It is not only the constitutional monarch who has a responsibility 'to advise, to encourage and to warn'.

Hume was second to none in his ability to 'warn' when he felt warning to be appropriate. But he was never slow with encouragement.

Perhaps the greatest test came in 1991–92 when several hundred Anglican priests expressed the wish to become Roman Catholic priests in the wake of the decision by the Church of England to ordain women. Hume exercised consummate sensitivity and succeeded in maintaining good relationships with the Anglican hierarchy.

In April 1999 it was announced that Cardinal Hume was suffering from terminal cancer but intended to 'carry on as usual' for as long as he could. When he entered hospital six weeks later those closest to him must have quickly become aware that the illness was unlikely to be prolonged. To the rest of the country the news of his death on 17 June came as an unexpected and grievous blow.

When Hume left Ampleforth for Westminster in 1976 he expressed 'profound shock' at receiving over one thousand letters and four hundred telegrams. The announcement of his illness and death provoked many thousands of letters, a large number of them beginning 'I am not a believer ...' The *Times* obituary stated that 'Few churchmen this century, inside or outside the Catholic Church, have died more deeply loved'.

Why was the country so saddened by the death of this man? Part of the answer must lie in the radiant humility that shone out upon a world thirsting for holiness. A lifelong friend, Dom Benedict Webb, describes Basil Hume as 'wearing his sanctity on his sleeve'.

A few weeks before his death Cardinal Hume had been appointed to the Order of Merit, one of the highest honours in the personal gift of the monarch. His funeral was virtually a state occasion. The Queen was represented by the Duchess of Kent, and others attending included the Archbishop of Canterbury, the Prime Ministers of the UK and of Ireland, the Leader of the Opposition and prominent men and women from all walks of life. Perhaps this is an indication that, as well as being greatly loved, Basil Hume in fact exercised a far-reaching influence well beyond the confines of his own church, the true extent of which may never be publicly acknowledged.

TERESA DE BERTODANO

FATHER, SON AND HOLY SPIRIT

*Every word that you find in the Gospel
is directed to you personally, and if
by flight of fancy or imagination you
were the only person who ever existed,
then the Lord would have become man,
and the Gospel would have been
written, just for you.*

UNPUBLISHED

A very precious way to pray is just through silence. No thoughts or words, just wanting to be silent in the presence of God. Perhaps one of the high points in prayer is where two silences meet: God's silence and our silence. No need for thoughts – and words get in the way.

MYSTERY OF LOVE, p. 33

*I*t was Chesterton who remarked that when we cease to believe in God then we start believing in anything.

MYSTERY OF THE INCARNATION, p. 51

*H*ow important it is always to have in the back of our minds, to be able to bring to the front in time of need, the great conviction of God's very special care and interest in each one of us.

UNPUBLISHED

*A*lways see the Gospel like a personal love letter from the Lord to yourself.

UNPUBLISHED

*A*n admirable way of praying the Gospel or, better, of using the Gospel as prayer, is to read a passage slowly. Whenever the name 'Jesus' occurs, or 'he', referring to 'Jesus', then change 'Jesus' or 'he' to 'You' and change the person to whom Our Lord is speaking to 'me'. In this way your reading of the Gospel becomes a conversation between Our Lord and you. Is not this what it is meant to be? Try it with the account of the blind man being cured, in St Luke's Gospel (Luke 18:35-43).

TO BE A PILGRIM, p. 128

*W*e must always seek the God who gives consolations and not ask or seek the consolations of God.

TO BE A PILGRIM, p. 138

'*T*he eagle flies over its little ones; without pressing heavily upon them it glides, touching them and not touching them.' [2] This image of the eagle hovering above the nest is a beautiful one. The transcendence and majesty of God does not impose, does not smother us, but invites and beckons us to open our hearts and to feed on his love.

REMAKING EUROPE, p. 23

A man who afterwards became a prominent
Christian said that his idea of God was revolutionised
when as a little boy he was taken to visit an old lady.
The old lady pointed out to him a text on her wall:
'Thou, God, seest me', and she said to him: 'You see
those words, they do not mean God is always watching
you to see what you are doing wrong, they mean he
loves you so much that he cannot take his eyes off you.'

MYSTERY OF THE INCARNATION, p. 91

*W*e can have all kinds of thoughts about our Father,
but we need to go beyond the thoughts of the Person
of the Father. We speak to him, present to us, but we
are hopelessly let down by our senses. We do not see,
hear, smell or touch him. We are just aware that he is
near us, and we want him to be close to us and us to
him. The more we go on in the dark, as if sitting with
him in a darkened room, the more we shall become
aware of his presence.

TO BE A PILGRIM, pp. 130-1

*T*here is one place where Christ wishes to rule, which he wishes to dominate, to make his own, to have no rivals, and that's in our hearts. That's where he wants to rule.

UNPUBLISHED

*T*ouching is very important. It is a way of speaking. Sometimes when we touch we can say more than with words. Touching is a way of showing love … Our Lord used touch. He touched people when they were blind and gave them sight. He touched a person who was deaf and could not speak, and in that way enabled him to talk. He touched the leper and cured him.

UNPUBLISHED

I doubt whether the Corinthians were a particularly impressive community; rather the contrary. St Paul did not tell the Corinthians that holiness was for other people. And he would certainly not dispense us from the effort to become more Christ-like.

TO BE A PILGRIM, p. 108

I know there's always the danger of reading into the Scriptures what you want to find, and it's also very easy to be put off by the fact that we've been told by the scholars that it doesn't really mean this or mean that. But my vision of the old father, as I like to think of it, is that his prodigal son had slipped away and squandered all his inheritance, and I like to think (transposing cultures and all the rest of it) of the old man slipping down to the gate of his garden every day, perhaps several times a day, just on the off chance that his beloved son might be on his way home. And that, to my way of thinking, is what God is like.

UNPUBLISHED

*G*od cannot count. Everybody is number one. God became man not for a crowd but for each one of us.

UNPUBLISHED

*P*erhaps the most fundamental freedom we possess is that of choosing how we respond to God's love.

REMAKING EUROPE, p. 23

*T*he Jewish Passover is a marvellous mixture of informality and solemnity; serious prayer, laughter and much conversation. That happened at the Last Supper, and it got heated as they quarrelled about who would be the greatest in the kingdom of heaven. Idle talk. So Our Lord had to make the point: 'Tell me', he asked, 'which is the greater, the man who sits at the table or the man who serves him?' So he got up and washed their feet to show that humble service of others is what matters.

UNPUBLISHED

*A*n excellent way of praying is to use phrases from the Gospels, and repeat them slowly again and again. Such prayers as: 'Lord, be merciful to me a sinner'; 'Lord, I do believe; help thou my unbelief'; 'Lord, thou knowest all things, thou knowest that I love thee'; 'Lord, to whom should I go? Thou hast the words of eternal life'; 'Thy will be done, not mine'; 'Speak, Lord, thy servant listeneth'. The Gospels are full of examples of this kind of prayer.

TO BE A PILGRIM, p. 127

*R*eligion without the love of God is cold and unreal, it becomes burdensome, and then there is the danger of rejecting it. How often has religion been rejected, jettisoned, because it weighed upon our spirit instead of releasing it?

To Be a Pilgrim, p. 125

*W*e so often distort the concept of love. We caricature the reality; we deface it; we think of it as a weak, rather insipid, emotion. But the love of which Our Lord speaks is demanding. It is a giving experience, selfless and generous. Love wants to give, as much as it wants to receive, and its model and prototype is the love that is in God.

To Be a Pilgrim, p. 123

*H*ow much we need Our Lord to touch our eyes so that we may see more clearly; to touch our ears that we may listen more acutely; to touch our limbs to give strength and purpose to our step.

Light in the Lord, p. 125

Our Lord had been speaking to his followers about 'the bread of life' and, at one point, had said: 'My flesh is real food, my blood is real drink.' That was hard to understand, and harder still to accept. It is not surprising that we then read: 'After this many of his disciples went back to their old ways, and walked no more in his company.' That was a blow to Jesus. 'Would you, too, go away?' he asked the twelve (John 6:67).

We, too, may at times be tempted 'to walk no more in his company'. But if we do that, then we walk alone into the darkness.

To Be a Pilgrim, p. 119

If you are troubled, sometimes, by doubts, and your mind cannot rise above the testimony of your senses, if your faith in the real presence of Christ in the Eucharist has grown weak, then try this. Kneel before the Blessed Sacrament, and say: 'My Lord and my God. I do believe; help thou my unbelief.' It works. And, then, reflect that in this, as in so many things concerned with God, understanding comes with practice. We get involved first, and then we begin to see the point.

To Be a Pilgrim, p. 146

*T*o understand and speak about the kingdom of God
it is necessary to keep four aspects of that kingdom in
mind. The kingdom of God is present now; it is at the
same time a future reality. It is internal to the hearts
and minds of the baptised; it is at the same time an
external reality in the world. To emphasise one aspect
and to neglect the others is to present an incomplete
picture of the kingdom and can lead us badly astray; it
can give a distorted view of the role of the Church in
the world.

To Be a Pilgrim, p. 199

*I*t is only recently that I have understood that
irrespective of whether I have the taste to spend time
alone with the Lord in prayer, he in fact wants my
time given just for him, my undivided attention
(it will rarely be undivided, for distractions and often
unwelcome visitors will crowd into my mind). I may
not want to give time to prayer. He does. Surely that
is the meaning of those well-known words: 'He came
to the disciples and found them sleeping; and he said
to Peter, "So, could you not watch with me one hour?
Watch and pray …"' (Matt. 26:40-1).

Light in the Lord, p. 115

*I*t would seem odd – or at least it would seem so to me – if people who must go to work each day and must care for families cannot, through these activities, achieve a high degree of holiness and be very close to God. If it is not possible, then the hidden life of Our Lord at Nazareth would make little sense, and the values and precepts of the Gospel would be meaningless. It cannot be. Once God is put at the centre of a life, then the rest follows.

In Praise of Benedict, p. 78

*T*here is a great deal of talk these days about 'why do we call God our Father, why not our mother?' It is about the feminine in God. God is neither man nor woman. What you find in man, in a different way you find in God and what you find in woman you find in God: those deep characteristics which make one different from the other, yet the one complementing the other. In God I will find infinite tenderness and I find that immensely encouraging and immensely stimulating. God is the most tender of all as well as being the strongest of all.

Unpublished

Sometimes I find myself praying as the leper prayed: 'If it be your will, Lord, you can make me clean.' Or like the blind man on the way to Jericho: 'Lord, that I may see.' Or like the paralytic who had to be let down through the roof because there was no other access to Our Lord, I pray that I may have my legs restored that I may walk more courageously, with a more determined step in the pilgrimage through life. Or like that deaf mute waiting to have my ears opened so that I can truly hear the word of God, listen to the message he is trying to give; and having heard and listened carefully, then have my tongue loosened to be able to sing his praises.

MILLENNIUM LENTEN MEDITATIONS

Pentecost is now. The Spirit is constantly at work in the Church and in the world.

REMAKING EUROPE, p. 35

The yearning for a direct encounter with God is a precious gift; it is part of God's enduring and transforming presence in the world.

REMAKING EUROPE, p. 42

'Why should I rejoice?' you might say. It is my life's experience that there is no day on which I shall keep from tears and not know sadness or misfortune. I weep bitter tears for myself when my mind knows only anguish and anxiety, my body pain and fatigue. If God be the goodness which is claimed for him, if he has that love for us which no human love can match, then why does evil seem to rule our hearts and hold sway in his creation? Yet his message is still: 'Rejoice, do not be afraid.'

TO BE A PILGRIM, p. 73

Not for me
to read the mind of God,
nor to pronounce on his ways.
Much is hidden
little revealed.
And yet,
though hard at times to see,
love is his reason,
this
and only this
inspires his deeds.

UNPUBLISHED

*H*owever much we may feel ourselves to be failures, and failures in God's eyes, we can always pray: 'God, be merciful to me a sinner.' You will remember the comment made by Our Lord about the tax-collector's prayer: 'I tell you, this man went down into his house justified rather than the other; because everyone that exalts himself shall be humbled, and he that humbles himself shall be exalted.' The tax-collector hated his sin. His prayer for forgiveness included the will to try to overcome his sinfulness.

To Be a Pilgrim, p. 70

*T*here is an ancient story about St Augustine, theologian and great Father of the Church. It relates how one day, walking along the beach, he saw a small boy who, having dug a hole in the sand, was running to and from the sea pouring water into it with his shell. Asked what he was doing he answered: 'I'm going to put the whole ocean into this hole.' When told that was impossible he replied: 'It is easier to put the whole ocean into this hole than for you to under-stand the Mystery of the Trinity.'

Mystery of Love, p. 3

*W*e need to see the unbreakable connection between love of God and love of our neighbour.

TO BE A PILGRIM, p. 192

A warm and friendly fire is an image of God … Anyone who has wandered away from God should think of coming back into the warmth, that is, into the love he offers. There is warmth awaiting us all.

BASIL IN BLUNDERLAND, pp. 48, 50

*I*t is the role of the Holy Spirit to give light to the mind and warmth to our hearts. So when we receive the Holy Spirit at baptism or confirmation, it is to help us to understand the things of God better and to love him more. We also receive a kind of spiritual energy which makes us want to serve God and our neighbour, and to do so. It is grace working within us.

BASIL IN BLUNDERLAND, p. 50

CREATOR AND

REDEEMER

*Behind every Crucifix, hidden, for we
cannot see him, stands our Risen Lord.
Hidden in every suffering and pain is
the joy of closer union with him. His is
the victory. He invites us to share it.*

MYSTERY OF LOVE, p. 47

*S*t John says: 'Anyone who fails to love can never have known God, for God is love' (1 John 4:8). So all those times, when we have been drawn to others by the goodness and lovableness which we have discovered in them, are precious experiences. They are hints given to us by God of the way he thinks about us, of the way he regards us. Thus, two lovers are especially privileged to be able to explore together the meaning of the love of God.

To Be a Pilgrim, p. 124

*W*ithout God human life remains an enigma. The deepest hopes and desires of the human heart remain unfulfilled.

To Be a Pilgrim, p. 159

*T*he secrets, slowly discovered by us, are known to the Creator. Our discoveries are explorations of his mind. Those who are close to nature are more likely to be humble before it.

To Be a Pilgrim, p. 206

I want someone to know me completely, to understand me entirely, and to want me unconditionally. I want to be somebody's first choice, and I think the only one who knows me completely, understands me entirely, and wants me unconditionally, is God – and I am his first choice; and you are his first choice. The marvellous thing about God is that he cannot have second choices. He is limited that way! We are all first choices. God never sees crowds, he just sees the individuals.

LIGHT IN THE LORD, p. 77

*B*e sure of this: we shall not find the answers to the riddles of life other than in Christ, the wisdom of God.

IN PRAISE OF BENEDICT, p. 43

*I*t was on Mount Tabor that Christ was transfigured. Peter said on that occasion: 'It is good, Lord, for us to be here.' It is always a privilege to join Christ in his agony in the Garden. But it does hurt.

BASIL IN BLUNDERLAND, p. 33

*T*he wise men who came from the East were learned, and men of high position. But their wisdom and their learning enabled them to stoop and be small in the presence of a Child whom they recognised to be greater than they. They had humility; that is why they knelt and gave their gifts; their gifts expressed their humility.

To Be a Pilgrim, pp. 67-8

*S*ome people spend a lot of time looking back on their lives, others spend time daydreaming about the future, but the important moment is 'now'. In any present moment we can meet God. At any moment we can just think about God and send a quick message up to him. It may be a fleeting thought or a word spoken. For instance, I can just say 'I am trying to love you', or 'please help me', or 'I am sorry about this or that'. The present moment is always precious. Like a sacrament it is a meeting point between God and ourselves.

Basil in Blunderland, p. 25

*H*umankind is but slowly attuning itself to the rhythms and laws of nature.

Unpublished

*I*t is my experience that men and women of true eminence and real wisdom often have a deep humility. They know their own limitations and how much they do not know. It is good to meet a very learned but wise person, and to find in that person the wonder and simplicity of a child.

TO BE A PILGRIM, p. 67

*F*or two thousand years we have pondered the significance of the incarnation. I am certain that it still has power to transform our understanding of human nature, although historically we have constantly failed to live out its consequences.

REMAKING EUROPE, p. 69

*W*hen I doubt the meaning of life, its purpose and its point, I remember those golden words on the cross: 'I thirst' and I pray: 'Lord, remember me when you come into your kingdom.'

Those marvellous words addressed to you and me: 'I thirst for you.'

UNPUBLISHED

What shall we give,
you and I,
to him who thirsts for us?

A sweet cooling drink –
we call it love –
to quench the thirst
of him who first
loved us.

UNPUBLISHED

We belong to a Church that has not suffered in recent times as the Church in Eastern Europe and in the Third World often has. We have become a slightly spoiled and pampered Church compared with many others. Yet it is still possible for us to create a spirituality and asceticism of the cross without the pressure of external persecution or hardship. We have to see through the allure of consumerism and materialism and gear ourselves for the pressures of pilgrimage.

TO BE A PILGRIM, pp. 210-1

*T*he candle tells of the light of Christ, which we must be, whether active in the mission of the Church, or missionary in the Church through prayer and suffering.

UNPUBLISHED

*O*nce while preaching in a parish, I suddenly caught sight of a young mother with her child and you could see the love between them. I was terribly tempted to say to the congregation: 'Forget what I am saying and look over there, and you will see what we mean to God!'

LIGHT IN THE LORD, p. 76

*T*here is surely deep in the heart of each one of us a wanting and a needing of God, and that wanting and needing of God in us is only there because he himself wants and needs us. We could never begin to love God or understand what that might mean if he had not first loved us. Why God should want and need us is a mystery. But it is true: otherwise he would not have created us and life ultimately would have no meaning for us.

SEARCHING FOR GOD, pp. 99-100

*J*udas, oh Judas –
betrayal hurts more
when the one who betrays
has received much
from the one he betrays –
betrayal hurts
hurts very much.

UNPUBLISHED

*I*n quiet moments, when reflecting on suffering
and pain, I think it a bit 'over the top' to identify
my minor aches and pains with the passion of Christ.
Then I remind myself that nothing is too small or
insignificant in the eyes of God. Mine may be a very
light cross to carry, but it is still the cross, and happily
I know that Christ comes to help me carry it as once
Simon of Cyrene helped him.

BASIL IN BLUNDERLAND, p. 70

*R*ead, for example, in prayerful spirit, the story of that shepherd who left – a bit irresponsibly, I think – ninety-nine sheep to seek out the stray. Does that not reassure you as to just how precious you are? And does not that word show that it never was a case of our seeking God in the first place? He seeks us first. He will find us if we listen to his voice calling to us through the fog that often surrounds us.

UNPUBLISHED

*O*n Christmas Day in 1914, in the first year of the First World War, the ordinary soldiers facing each other in the trenches refused to fire and instead walked out into no man's land to sing carols, to exchange their rations and cigarettes. It was their tribute to the Child Jesus – the Christ who is our peace. The next year, I am told, the military authorities were ready and when a soldier who tried to repeat that Christmas truce went out into no man's land he was shot by his own officers.

MYSTERY OF THE INCARNATION, p. 89

*E*ver since I was a boy Christmas has meant for me Midnight Mass, all the trimmings of a family celebration and hospital. The reason for that final, perhaps unusual element, is that my father, who was a doctor, would bring the whole family to the Infirmary in Newcastle to help to serve the Christmas dinner. I've always been grateful to both my parents for letting me see from the start that Christmas is for sharing.

UNPUBLISHED

*T*o see this child,
in swaddling clothes
lying in a manger
is to see God himself.
It is not the Godhead directly
but God made man for us,
his manhood hiding and revealing
at the same time
the God that he is,
him in whom
we live and move
and have our being.

UNPUBLISHED

*E*very year,
at this time
we are asked
to escape from the tumult of our hearts
to put aside our weighty cares
and leave our wearisome toil,
to enter for a while
into the inner chamber of our souls,
to listen to his word.

The Word –
calling us
through the mist
of ignorance and apathy
to be silent,
to listen
to the sound of stillness,
and so to see
in the child born of Mary
the Word who became flesh.

UNPUBLISHED

It is possible to refuse to go to him. It is possible to deny him, to adore not him but false gods, to hate him even. We can walk away deliberately. We can choose self, self alone, above and before all. We shall live lonely, barren, empty, miserable lives. That is hell.

To Be a Pilgrim, p. 229

If your heart is in pain or your body,
if your burden is too great,
if visited by anguish,
almost broken,
then open yourself to him.
He will come, if you ask
and he will dwell within,
he the Word made flesh for you.

UNPUBLISHED

God is like the sun; we cannot see him as he is. We need someone to tell us about him, someone who knows and who can be trusted to speak the truth. Our Lord knows, and he has spoken to us.

To Be a Pilgrim, p. 118

*R*ight down the ages we can say that history is the story of our failure to love.

To Be a Pilgrim, p. 125

*S*ome people say that in the artist's work you will see something of the artist, and for me this is the closest and best analogy. If you look at a work of art you will always see something of the artist. Some people can recognise composers: that is Mozart, for example, or that is Beethoven. We leave part of ourselves in what we create, and that is a simple thought about God: he has left part of himself in his creation. It is through *that* that we can build up our picture of what God is like.

Mystery of the Cross, p. 47

*I*f you have never been through darkness, then you simply cannot speak to people about the light. If you have never been through doubt you probably cannot speak eloquently about faith. You have to know that side of life – the crucifixion side, the passion side – in order to be able to speak eloquently about the resurrection side.

Light in the Lord, p. 133

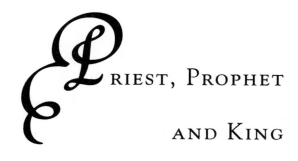

PRIEST, PROPHET AND KING

Each baptised person is anointed, as Christ was, priest, prophet and king. In the body of Christ which is the Church, the baptised person shares in this threefold function of the Head of the body. The 'ordinary Catholic' – if the phrase has to be used – has then a remarkable dignity. This baby, just baptised, is in some wonderful manner, priest, prophet and king; this lapsed Catholic who has strayed far from the Church, cannot cease to be priest, prophet and king.

TO BE A PILGRIM, p. 193

*T*he word 'Church' is used by most to mean the institutional Church and then, specifically, its leadership, Pope, bishops, priests and religious. Only rarely do people remember that Church means also the whole community, the laity as well as the clergy.

To Be a Pilgrim, p. 163

*W*e somehow have to make the celebration of the Eucharist attractive. We will not do it by making it consciously cheerful. We will not do it by eccentric celebrations. But the secret is to go deeper into the meaning. It is easier to say that than to know how to do it. But I think that once we realise that 'actuosa participatio' means participating at a very deep level, at a prayerful level, and become involved in the whole mystery of Christ, we might then have begun to discover its richness. But when we try to make it superficially interesting and exciting, we bore people.

Light in the Lord, pp. 105-6

*T*he harvest is riper than we know, and we need labourers for the reaping.

To Be a Pilgrim, p. 210

*A*sk any young person what they think about the Mass, and you know the answer: 'It's boring.' Have you ever persuaded a young person that it is not? Mind you, they are equally likely to dismiss many of life's richest and most enduring experiences in exactly the same way. Nonetheless, our forefathers appreciated the Mass, loved the Mass, died for it. And our people instinctively know this is important.

LIGHT IN THE LORD, p. 105

*M*any people listening to us do not want to know what we know, they want to know what faith means to us. It only means something to us to the degree that we are people of prayer.

LIGHT IN THE LORD, p. 117

*H*ow much power there is in the hands of ordinary decent people when they are seized by a vision, however dimly perceived.

TO BE A PILGRIM, p. 179

I have often thought that Our Lord chose a lot of 'Division Two' people as priests. We can all think of better people among the laity than ourselves, and we all know our frailties and our weaknesses. I sometimes think he has deliberately chosen the earthenware vessels to be quite certain that the strays and failures will have someone who will understand and be sympathetic, and not condemn. For who of us would dare to condemn others when we know our real selves? So he made those who were going to be shepherds of his flock themselves rather frail precisely so that they could have sympathy and compassion in order to help the lost sheep.

LIGHT IN THE LORD, p. 61

*H*ow many times do people walk away from the Church because Father barked at them? One of the things that makes me fear and tremble is how many people have I sent away because I 'barked' on the telephone, was not gentle, or did not listen?

LIGHT IN THE LORD, p. 80

*E*ach time I put the question at an ordination about exercising 'the ministry of the Word worthily and wisely' I am made to think very hard about my own role as a teacher. How well do I carry out this duty? Am I really a 'witness' by the way I live? Is there real conviction in my voice as I speak? Have I personally been affected by the Word of God? Has it changed me? Our listeners want not only to hear what we have to say, but what it means to us. Our congregations are quick to detect how genuine we are. If we are men of prayer, then our words will touch hearts as well as minds. When we pray, faith is alive; when faith is active and not dormant our words speak.

LIGHT IN THE LORD, pp. 66-7

*O*ur people know when we are witnesses as well as teachers. I always remember listening with horror to a priest whose sermon from the point of view of sheer delight in the construction of words and images could not be faulted; it was absolutely brilliant. But it was dead, because that priest was going through terrible troubles and living a double life. You could just sense it. We have to be witnesses if we are going to be good teachers.

LIGHT IN THE LORD, p. 67

The essence of the priesthood is a living relationship with Christ. A living relationship with Christ is fostered and enveloped by a 'life of prayer'. A priest who has ceased to pray and who no longer develops his understanding of the Word of God cannot effectively give to the world hungry for the things of God what it should rightly expect from him.

Consciously make space each day for prayer no matter what the other pressures and demands of your ministry. You will find that in everyday living prayer can easily be given less time and effort and then possibly be discarded. That would be a disastrous loss.

LIGHT IN THE LORD, p. 115

If the priest who should represent the principle of reconciliation and unity in the community becomes too directly and personally involved in the political process, he runs the risk of dividing his community and unnecessarily antagonising some of its members. His public stance on political matters which should properly be left to the initiative and concern of the laity may have the effect of driving some people out of the Church in anger and protest.

TO BE A PILGRIM, p. 166

*H*ave I the heart of a priest? Is my heart in my priest-hood? Or has my treasure become something other than my priesthood? Do I sense still a certain thrill as I go to the altar to celebrate Mass, or is it a bit different now? Do I long to speak to the people of the good news of the Gospel, or has it become dull and uninter-esting for me, and thus uninteresting when I speak about it? Do I love the sick and the poor? Does my priestly heart still feel for those in distress? Do I feel awe and reverence for the Blessed Sacrament, or has familiarity – or, worse still, doubt – coloured my atti-tude? Do I still feel a terrible humility and awesome responsibility as I say in the confessional: 'I absolve you from your sins …'?

To Be a Pilgrim, p. 212

*T*he liturgy will often be 'ghastly' and 'boring', but then we must ask ourselves a question. Do we go to Mass in our parish church in order to be entertained or in some way to be fulfilled? Or do we go because it is important to be there, and to contribute our best to the praising and worship of God, and for his sake and not ours?

Basil in Blunderland, p. 42

I think that one of my chief anxieties is the welfare and happiness of priests, and I believe that my first responsibility is to look after, to care for the priests.

LIGHT IN THE LORD, p. 142

*M*any Catholics regard participation in the life of the Church as being a responsibility 'to help the priest': 'Just tell us what to do, Father, and we'll be there.' There is still much to be done to enable people to understand how their incorporation into the life of Christ gives them a direct share in his mission.

TOWARDS A CIVILISATION OF LOVE, p. 126

*W*e should think of our parish liturgy as 'the tuning of the instruments' preparing for the perfect song of praise when we shall be in the very presence of God and see him face to face. It will be a song of praise in tune, melodious and just a delight to be involved. I won't wince any more, when the music jars and the hymns seem to me to be banal. Anyway, I don't sing in tune, so why should I be so critical of others. Forgive me, Lord.

BASIL IN BLUNDERLAND, p. 42

I never cease to be amazed, whenever I have anything to do with television, by the meticulous care
taken in preparing programmes. The producers go on
trying until they get it right. I ask myself: 'How well
do I prepare for the Mass I am about to celebrate?' It is
so important how we, the celebrants, do our part, as it
is for the readers and singers to do theirs. Our people
should leave the Masses we celebrate having sensed
the presence of God.

LIGHT IN THE LORD, p. 106

*T*oo many people have been 'sacramentalised' but
not 'evangelised'.

REMAKING EUROPE, p. 79

*I*t is my firm belief that people today are hungry.
They may not know what they are hungry for, but they
are hungry: hungry for truth about life as a whole, and
hungry for truth about their own lives and the meaning of them. They want to be told things that will give
them strength, comfort and a sense of direction. They
need to know what will make life worth living.

TO BE A PILGRIM, p. 209

*C*ardinal Cardijn, that great apostle of the workers, used to say: 'No work – no Mass.' It was his way of getting working people to see that their efforts made life possible and helped to shape the offering we make at each Mass. Builders construct the church; quarry-men bring the stone for the altar; miners dig the coal which fuels power-stations for heat and light; weavers make the linen for the vestments and the altar-cloths; farmers produce the wheat for the bread and the grapes for the wine; public transport workers and the car-plant men make it possible for the congregation to gather. All in their own way, through their work, make the Mass possible.

To Be a Pilgrim, p. 207

*T*he Church is described, to take only a few examples, as a 'sheepfold', as 'a choice vineyard', and quite astonishingly, as 'the Body of Christ' and equally remarkably as his 'bride'. All this suggests a remarkable intimacy that should obtain between ourselves and Christ, and following from this and because of it, with each other.

Light in the Lord, p. 153

*T*here comes a moment, which we can never quite locate or catch, when an acquaintance becomes a friend. In a sense, the change from one to the other has been taking place over a period of time, but there comes a point when we know that we can trust the other, exchange confidences, keep each other's secrets. We are friends.

There has to be a moment like that in our relationship with God. He ceases to be just a Sunday acquaintance, and becomes a weekday friend.

To Be a Pilgrim, p. 109

*I*t is clear that the most important and characteristic feature of Christ's teaching on marriage was his insistence on its permanence, on the lifelong commitment of husband and wife to each other. 'What God has united, man must not divide.' He was not formulating a set of precepts to impose on married people; instead he focused on what he saw as the given reality. He saw what human love is and can be, and teaches how marriage can best express that love and prevent it from being spoiled or abused.

To Be a Pilgrim, p. 201

*A*lthough there is in the Church a sacrament of marriage, religion did not invent marriage. It is not the preserve of Jew or Christian; it is the heritage of all humanity.

It is a pity that most pastoral and professional attention is directed towards marriages in crisis. If we are concerned exclusively with the care of the sick, we may ignore the needs of the healthy and that is the quickest way to swell the ranks of the sick. Most marriages last and are happy, but all marriages could be better. This is too important to be left to chance. We cannot simply celebrate a wedding service and then leave couples to their own resources. We need to support and sustain families at every stage of their development, but especially in the early years. When stress nevertheless develops, and breakdown occurs, the Church recognises and claims its proper role, namely that of healing without reproach.

It is important always to be firm on principle, but compassionate towards individuals.

To Be a Pilgrim, pp. 201, 202

I met some time ago a woman in her seventies. She has had and is having a dreadful life (she is not a Catholic) – a *dreadful* life with a cantankerous and, I would say, somewhat unbalanced husband. She said: 'I could leave him, Father, I could; but I won't because of my vows.' Such was her loyalty and devotion to a promise, made some fifty years ago, which had brought her little pleasure, little joy.

SEARCHING FOR GOD, p. 132

*T*he patience, courage, cheerfulness, spirituality of those who suffer often give more to us than we can give to them.

TO BE A PILGRIM, p. 219

*W*e are neither wiser nor better than our forefathers. If the Christian philosophy of life based on respect and love for God and for our neighbours had been embraced and practised throughout the world, then the terrible crimes of our age could never have been perpetrated.

TO BE A PILGRIM, p. 35

*A*s a family, we live in his name and for his purposes, so Christ is in our midst. When we break bread together we are both expressing our unity and strengthening it.

IN PRAISE OF BENEDICT, p. 47

*W*hen you really love, nothing is too menial, nothing is too monotonous, nothing too trivial.

SEARCHING FOR GOD, p. 68

*M*en and women need both vision and hope if they are to set about building the kingdom of God. That vision and hope are given to them by God's revelation.

TO BE A PILGRIM, p. 177

*W*e Christians have to realise just how much we have to give, simply because we are baptised. Our solidarity with Christ is deepened each time we receive him in Holy Communion.

TO BE A PILGRIM, p. 47

The towns and cities of our land are full of people who do not need our silver and gold, but desperately need to hear the good news of the Gospel. They are lame and crippled without God. They perish because they do not have any vision about life and its meaning and about the right way to find happiness. They need to know, they need to experience that there is a God who loves them.

TO BE A PILGRIM, p. 47

When I was young my faith was 'over there' and I was here. I knew it to be important but it wasn't yet here, inside, and I came to realise much later in life that there is a process whereby we grow into spiritual maturity, when faith becomes part of me and not outside me. I look back on my adolescent years as years not only when faith was there and I was here, but also of considerable muddle and confusion inside. That is natural and inevitable because in all growth there must of necessity be growing pains, problems and difficulties. That is the law of growth.

UNPUBLISHED

A long time ago I had a friend who had been born blind. He had one great enthusiasm in his life and that was watching cricket. He had no idea what cricket looked like. Yet he had this tremendous interest, almost a passion for it. I used to take him to matches, sit beside him, giving a running commentary. He would be riveted and get very excited.

The point is this: he was totally dependent on what I was saying to him. I could have been telling him a pack of lies. We might not even have been watching a cricket match at all. But, no, as I described the game he got more and more interested and involved.

It was that experience that taught me about faith … You and I depend entirely on what God tells us. That is why the Word of God is so important. Faith is listening to what God has to say through the Scriptures.

MYSTERY OF LOVE, p. 8

*K*neeling before the priest confessing humbly our sins, trying hard to be sorry and receiving God's forgiveness, is a great help to growing in holiness.

TO BE A PILGRIM, p. 113

*A*lways start your leadership where people are and lead them to where they didn't dream they might go. So often, we do not start where people are and we expect things from people that they are not able to give.

In the Church today, I am constantly being urged to suppress this group of people or that group of people, drive out this lot or that lot … And I will not do it simply because one has to lead them from where they are to where you think they should be. If you drive a person or people out you don't do the Church any good.

UNPUBLISHED

*G*od seeks always
to forgive,
he will look for every reason
to forgive
to make excuses for us,
to understand.

UNPUBLISHED

*P*ublic prayer finds its real soul when we start doing seriously private prayer.

MYSTERY OF LOVE, p. 32

*W*e should never allow ourselves to be overwhelmed by our unworthiness, our sinfulness: we must always cling to the thought that God is incapable – if I may put it this way – of exercising his wonderful power of forgiveness if there is nothing to forgive. Our sinfulness is a claim on his power of forgiveness which is part of his loving concern.

SEARCHING FOR GOD, p. 206

*I*n the Eucharist, which is summit and source of all our life in Christ's body, the scattered human race is gathered together and all creation is bound with it into a single offering to the Father of all that is. Our world is thus made holy and given back to God. It is a foretaste and promise of the everlasting banquet in the eternal kingdom.

TOWARDS A CIVILISATION OF LOVE, pp. 176-7

I sometimes think that it is harder for many people to believe that God loves them than to believe that he exists.

UNPUBLISHED

*G*enuine love of God and humanity is learnt in the desert. Learn it there and you will have something to sell in the market place – the pearl of great price.

SEARCHING FOR GOD, p. 39

*T*he kind of God we adore, is one who looks out always for us, wanting us to return constantly to him, and when he sees us takes pity on us, throws his arms round our neck and kisses us.

UNPUBLISHED

*L*ord, I want to see your beauty, your truth, your goodness. I want to know your understanding, to experience your forgiveness, and of course above all to know your love. I want to see your strength, the power that you are, to see you forgive and to have the consolation that you forgive me too, to see your tenderness which I have always needed.

UNPUBLISHED

In Praise of Benedict

Monks are ordinary people, on the whole.
We are not spiritually star performers.
So the Rule of St Benedict *makes it*
possible for ordinary folk to live lives of
quite extraordinary value. The weak
have a place to do their best …

In Praise of Benedict, p. 24

A good religious, if I may call on my own experience, receives his or her first novitiate in the family. The first lessons in prayer are not given in the seminary or novitiate; they are given in the home.

TO BE A PILGRIM, p. 217

*W*hen I was younger and gave retreats, I used to think my role was to tell other people how to behave and how to think. As you get older you grow out of that.

LIGHT IN THE LORD, p. 105

*I*f you want to be faithful to Christ, if you want to live seriously as a Christian, you are in for a struggle. It will often seem easier to turn round and run away.

TO BE A PILGRIM, p. 151

*E*very act, however small and unimportant, can be an act of love.

TO BE A PILGRIM, p. 203

*F*ind time in the day which you can, so to speak, waste with God; make it regular, and be faithful to it, however short it is and no matter how you are feeling. When prayer is not easy, and we do it nonetheless, we are proving that we are trying to love God. And if you stick at it, God will begin to speak to you – for, as you well know, it is he who is in fact in search of us. He wants us, and always more than we can ever want him.

In Praise of Benedict, p. 67

*W*e are 'earthenware vessels', frail and inadequate no doubt, but 'let us ask God that he be pleased, where our nature is powerless, to give us the help of his grace'.[3]

In Praise of Benedict, p. 9

*B*eing patient, tolerant, understanding – all that can cost a lot, as anyone who has lived in community can tell you. It is harder to endure being bored by someone else's conversation than to give up sugar in your tea or coffee!

To Be a Pilgrim, p. 115

*I*f you ask anyone who is knowledgable about Church matters, to name two or three Benedictines who are world-famous, he would probably not be able to get further than mentioning a name or two from some Benedictine community known to him. On the whole, monks do not become famous – and that is a good thing – but monasteries do – and that is an excellent thing. In other words, it is the community that matters. It is as a member of a community that the individual monk does his particular job.

IN PRAISE OF BENEDICT, p. 25

*T*hose most likely to make good and successful hermits will be those who have known how to live well in community.

IN PRAISE OF BENEDICT, p. 6

*S*o many people think that having a spiritual life means always being 'on a high'. In reality, for most people, a serious spiritual life involves going through darkness when faith is tried.

FOOTPRINTS OF THE NORTHERN SAINTS, p. 25

*D*uring the day things go wrong. For instance: you have been unfairly (or even fairly) criticised; you have been unjustly treated; you have been insulted or just ignored; someone has been unkind to you; you have been snubbed. Those are golden opportunities to grow in holiness. You will probably feel furious and want 'to get your own back'. Try this: bite your lips, as it were, and just say 'thanks be to God'. You will go on feeling furious, but that prayer, said when you are churned up and upset, is extraordinarily valuable and it does bring a deep peace – eventually.

To Be a Pilgrim, p. 111

*E*xperience has shown me that reflective praying – which we call meditation or mental prayer – is, for me, much better done early in the morning. As the day's affairs gather momentum, so our minds become increasingly cluttered – at least for most of us. Others prefer to pray in the evening after the day's work. Much depends on our temperaments as to which we find the easier.

Basil in Blunderland, p. 32

God never changes, is always quite still, but he is always very active, and creative all the time.

BASIL IN BLUNDERLAND, p. 48

Monks have many advantages: we are assured of three meals a day, we have a roof over our heads, we are clothed, we live in congenial company, we have security for our old age. There can only be one justification for our being given by God these wonderful things, these great advantages, when the majority of people do not share them. It can only be justified on the grounds that we are living a life that makes demands on us.

SEARCHING FOR GOD, p. 129

Forgive me, Lord, for my failures and shortcomings, but I know deep down that you use me as you find me, and in spite of myself. That is consoling, but give me, I pray, the heart of a priest, especially a heart that knows the meaning of true love, love of God and love of the people. May I be helped to translate that love into action and into service of others.

TO BE A PILGRIM, pp. 212-3

I would urge you to have the highest ambitions in your lives about your holiness. Don't accept to be average, don't accept to be less than the ideal; but without straining, without taking on great burdens, see in the circumstances of everyday life what God is trying to say to you, and go on trusting and thanking him, and be drawn closer and closer in your prayer lives to Our Lord Jesus Christ.

UNPUBLISHED

*A*s an abbot, I was always frightened when people said: 'Oh, the Abbot is terribly busy, we must not worry him.' That is not right. If the Abbot should be worried, then he must be.

SEARCHING FOR GOD, p. 118

*I*t is not where we are or what we do that matters; it is who we are and what we become.

TO BE A PILGRIM, p. 110

*D*on't take yourselves too seriously. Take *life* seriously. Take *God* seriously. But don't, please don't, take yourselves too seriously! ...

All the monks [at Ampleforth] are in some way wounded. You are joining a community composed of extremely imperfect human beings. It is rather like being in a hospital where the matron, as well as the patients, is sick! You are not entering a community of saints. If that is what you thought we were, then please go! ...

In any monastery if you look for things to criticise you will find enough to keep you busy all day. If you are sensitive and understanding, then you are in a position to make constructive and sensible suggestions.

SEARCHING FOR GOD, pp. 30, 35, 43

*T*here is nothing more dangerous, nor more hideous, than spiritual pride. It is a very subtle thing, and it can all too easily creep into our lives. When we despise others, think we are superior, feel satisfied with our spiritual effort – these are manifestations of spiritual pride.

TO BE A PILGRIM, p. 69

A life spent in trying to love God and our neighbour will be a happy life, and happy in proportion as we become more selfless. The wounded and the weak among us limp along, but deep down we can be at peace for we know that his love for us is stronger than our neglect of him.

TO BE A PILGRIM, p. 36

*I*n each [novice] there is a fundamental flaw which can be your undoing – of that there is no question. A flaw of this nature can lead us to make fools of ourselves, to make some grave mistake. To recognise this flaw and learn to cope with it is one of the ways of remaining in the monastic life.

Now it does not matter if you have faults, provided two factors remain unshakable. First, you should be devoted to prayer; you should *want* to pray – not emotionally but in your will … Secondly, you should genuinely want to belong to this community: to throw in your lot with us, despite your faults and weaknesses. You should be ready to face an unknown future – in the company of these men on their way through life in search of God.

SEARCHING FOR GOD, pp. 49-50

*F*ear of failure can be a crippling handicap.

TOWARDS A CIVILISATION OF LOVE, p. 79

I would much prefer a person to be disobedient than to whittle down obedience; much rather that one be honest and say: 'I am just jolly well not going to do it', than to whittle down the doctrine. I have come more and more to see just how central is obedience in the religious life. An obedient religious has acquired an interior freedom. Always see obedience as liberating, and a conforming to Christ …

Obedience is a defence against self-will: no wolf is cleverer at assuming sheep's clothing than the wolf of self-will.

SEARCHING FOR GOD, pp. 126, 44

*T*here should be in every monk a potential Trappist, a potential Carthusian – or, put it this way – there should be a little regret in each one of us that God did not call us to be a Carthusian: a regret that this great vocation was not offered to us.

SEARCHING FOR GOD, p. 146

*M*ost of our problems come from a lack of humility – the hardest quality to acquire, the most lovely to possess. Do not, I beg you, take yourself too seriously. Laugh at yourself. And let others laugh at you and with you. This is part of family life! ...

It is the essence of community life to want the happiness of others, to bring about their happiness, participate in their happiness; to avoid anything that might wound another, spoil a relationship, cloud mutual joy.

SEARCHING FOR GOD, pp. 216, 222

I believe that for some of us it is when we realise how little we are regarded by others that we begin to recognise how highly we are esteemed by God. We have ceased to wonder what others think about us; we have discovered our worth in the eyes of our Father ...

Only one thing matters, and that is what God thinks about me. To be high in his regard is the highest ambition any person can have.

TO BE A PILGRIM, pp. 67, 115

*T*he marvellous thing about becoming a superior is the discovery that everybody else is like me. They are all fragile and foolish and this is a wonderful thing. They are all as fragile as me. Surely that gives one a sense of compassion which a leader must always have.

UNPUBLISHED

I have often thought that the *Rule of St Benedict* was written for a monastery that functioned imperfectly. For instance, the *Rule* seems almost to assume that there will be misbehaviour in the oratory (*RSB* 52), that there will be late arrivals for prayer and for meals (*RSB* 43) and that complaints will be made about the quality of the clothes (*RSB* 55).

IN PRAISE OF BENEDICT, p. 9

*T*he gap between what is thought and expected of me, and what I know myself to be, is considerable and frightening. There are moments in life when a man feels very small, and in all my life this is one such moment. It is good to feel small, for I know that whatever I achieve will be God's achievement, not mine.[4]

SEARCHING FOR GOD, p. 237

I had a predecessor as Abbot [of Ampleforth] who was very close to God, and a great man of prayer. When he was told about the publication of Eugene Boylan's book *Difficulties in Mental Prayer* he remarked: 'It must be an awfully long book!' The reasons offered for not giving time to 'mental prayer' can be varied: 'It is too difficult', 'My work is my prayer', 'I have no time'.

LIGHT IN THE LORD, p. 117

*T*here are many tombs in this [Westminster] Abbey, but there is one which speaks, if we would listen, with a poignant, indeed tragic, eloquence. It is the tomb which contains the remains of two sisters, Elizabeth and Mary. Read, there, the inscription: 'Consorts both in throne and grave, here we rest, two sisters, Elizabeth and Mary, in the hope of one resurrection.' Think of them as you will, judge as you will, but pass on in your mind to the last phrase: 'in the hope of one resurrection'. New life springs up out of death. The sister Churches can now look back on a past that is dead and buried. We can look forward to new life, to new hope and in God's time to the goal of Christian unity.[5]

AMPLEFORTH JOURNAL, SUMMER 1976

*W*hen my predecessor [as Abbot] died at the age of ninety-four, the monk who wrote the obituary[6] made this striking observation: 'A man who bears a heavy burden, as he has done for so long, must live by the ethics of responsibility. He is the king who must keep the kingdom together rather than the prophet who can think in freedom, express his thoughts and damn the consequences.'

UNPUBLISHED

*I*f we are paralysed by 'inner hurts' we can turn inwards upon ourselves, and then we are unable to help others; or we are not free to be totally at the disposal of Christ. Yes, these inner wounds must be healed.

SEARCHING FOR GOD, p. 210

*A*s religious we ought to witness to love which is chaste, pure, right, above board and the rest of it. We have to rescue affection from being mixed up in everybody's mind with sex.

UNPUBLISHED

*A*s a young monk, looking at a very old breviary,
I found on its cover a picture of a crown of thorns
surrounding the word PEACE. Whatever is going on in
life, whatever pain, suffering or difficulties, there must
be peace at the centre. It occurred to me how important it is for us to have peace, a peace which is freedom
inside despite all the thorns of life. And, maybe, peace
inside, *because* of the thorns. To me, peace is like a rose
which is surrounded by thorns. In a manner they pro-
tect the rose, they contribute to it …

When you become an archbishop you have to take
a coat of arms. It is hardly among the priorities. I was
constantly being asked 'what motto I would adopt'.
I could not think of one. Then on Holy Saturday the
artist painting the shield wanted the motto that night.
I was rather angry because we had just had a lovely
ceremony, so, half jokingly, and rather irritated, I said:
'Put on it *Lumen Christi*' [Light of Christ]. We had just
sung 'Lumen Christi' several times. Later to my horror
I saw those words on the shield and wondered how a
bishop could claim to be 'Lumen Christi'! It seemed
arrogant beyond belief! I asked them to scrub it out
and replace it with *Pax Inter Spinas* [Peace Among the
Thorns].

LIGHT IN THE LORD, p. 152

*I*t was not easy to leave my monastery; it is never easy to leave home. The most difficult part was leaving all the people I had known for so long and had grown to love and respect. More than three hundred years ago a Frenchman wrote: 'Going away is a kind of dying.' So it is. There is pain and fear of the unknown, and a certain darkness threatening the spirit.

I know my experience is an everyday human experience. How much worse it is for those who have to leave their jobs, or who lose them, with all the uncertainty that can bring. I think of the man who has to leave his home and friends, and take his wife and family into the unknown. What a worry that can be; what darkness he may know, what uncertainty. This, and so much more, is the lot of millions of people today.

MYSTERY OF THE CROSS, p. 69

*T*here are no limits to God.

MYSTERY OF LOVE, p. 6

*Y*ou may not be in love with God, but God is most certainly in love with you. Always remember that. He has given you two tutors who will give you your first lessons in mature religious response. They are called love and pain. It is love which will attach you to God, and pain will detach you from exclusive entanglement with the goods of this world.

MYSTERY OF LOVE, p. 15

SEARCHING

FOR GOD

*Life is like a race. It begins and it ends.
In the race organised by God, everyone
wins. But – and this is quite essential –
you have to be involved in the race
otherwise you don't get a prize. In
God's world everyone is a winner.
But you must take part in the race.*

BASIL IN BLUNDERLAND, p. 9

Whether I work at an office desk, in the home, on the land or in a factory, my work is an act of love. So, in daily life, we do not witness to Jesus only when we speak about him but our work itself is a prayer. That is one reason why unemployment so grieves the Church and so invites its concern. Work is part of our humanity. Deprived of it, we feel ourselves threatened and devalued.

If we are seriously trying to live according to the mind of Christ, we will obviously want to throw ourselves wholeheartedly and with all our skills into our work. We will never be content merely to watch the clock and to regard employment simply as a means to pay the bills and have a good time. There will be legitimate pride in what we do. We will want to master our craft or our profession so as to give greater glory to God.

To Be a Pilgrim, p. 205

The daily round in the office, in the factory, at home, can lead to holiness, because holiness consists in doing ordinary things extraordinarily well.

To Be a Pilgrim, p. 203

*T*he values of the consumer society with its idols of wealth and power constitute a real danger to the Christian believer. They have been obstacles to faith right down the ages, and are as seductive today as at any time in the past. They can gradually coarsen the mind and the sensitivity of the believer. We gradually grow accustomed to the easy life and the pursuit of material goals. Ambition and reward become the inspiration of our lives.

TO BE A PILGRIM, p. 120

*T*oday many campaign vigorously for peace. Others work tirelessly for the protection of life from the time of conception to the end of life. Some are committed to providing housing for the homeless, to feeding the hungry, to protecting the environment. They are often prophets sent to the modern world. They are some-times uncomfortable people; quite often they are voices crying in the wilderness. Yet they are important people sent to remind us of difficult but necessary values.

TO BE A PILGRIM, p. 160

*T*he saints of Northumbria still live on in the north. I remember looking for the site where Edwin had his camp, near where Paulinus baptised. I remember walking up the hill and meeting a child of about eight. I asked her where the camp was and she pointed it out to me, and I asked her if she knew what happened there and she did. I asked if she had heard of so and so, and she said she had. I said, 'How do you know?' and she said they learnt it at school. I was very impressed. St Cuthbert is still alive in the north.

Footprints of the Northern Saints, p. 95

*P*rayer and suffering are the two indispensable tools, as it were, to make a holy person, to make a saint. Our Lord himself said you cannot be his follower unless you deny yourself, take up your cross and follow him. That applies to all of us. Whenever we undergo pain or suffering it is an imperative call from God to closer union with him. Suffering makes us think about what life is; it detaches us from the things of this world, and it purifies us.

Light in the Lord, p. 131

*F*reedom of choice is not an absolute value. The freedom we rightly cherish and enjoy has to be exercised according to the truth, not just according to our personal wishes.

UNPUBLISHED

*H*ave you ever instinctively disliked a person, until one day somebody tells you that person rather likes and admires you, and your attitude changes! But you warm to that person because you suddenly discover what you mean to them.

It is like that in our spiritual life. Once you begin to understand what you mean to God, then he begins to mean something to you.

UNPUBLISHED

*I*t is hard to die for ideals, but very noble. It is often even harder to live for ideals, and never to lose sight of that vision of what is desirable and good. To live for one's ideals requires dedication, and dedication demands selflessness, generosity, courage and tenacity. It must be expressed in deeds and not just in words.

TO BE A PILGRIM, p. 161

I once went to a dinner organised by the Variety Club of Great Britain. There were nine speakers and I was the ninth. I had a super speech but I did not write it. It was written by a little boy of ten who suffers from cerebral palsy. His name is Peter. He cannot speak at all but we made contact as best we could. One day through the auspices of the Variety Club he was given an electronic typewriter and within days of receiving it he wrote a poem which he sent to me:

I couldn't speak, I couldn't write,
I knew it wasn't right.
All the time I prayed one day to have a voice
And have my say.
They've made machines, now I can talk,
Tell stories and thank mum for her walks.
Tell dad I enjoyed his joke,
Explaining things to so many folk.
My thanks to you for making all my plans come true.

Perhaps this is not great poetry but it is a fantastic achievement. We, as priests, have so much to learn from people like Peter.

LIGHT IN THE LORD, pp. 80-1

$\mathcal{N}$o words can substitute for the actual experience of being close to those who are handicapped or suffering. Once, when visiting a hospital for mentally handicapped people, I was particularly struck when I went into a small ward of adolescents. They had been born blind, deaf, and mentally handicapped.

It takes an act of faith to be able to say, as St Thomas More said, 'Nothing can come but that which is God's will, and that indeed will be best.'

As I left that little ward, I could only reflect that one day I will see them again and that they will be the privileged among the loved ones of God. He sees in them a beauty which we cannot see. He has a plan for them which we cannot understand. Those born blind will one day open their eyes and, to their delight, the first thing they see will be the vision of the all-beautiful, God.

To Be a Pilgrim, pp. 220-1

Our Lord often met sick people and sinners, crocks and crooks. A prayerful study of how he handled them tells us much about the way God looks upon us in our weakness …

It is no bad thing to remain a 'crock' and in need of constant help. 'They that are in health need not a physician, but they that are ill' (Matt. 9:12). He has come for us. If you love a person you want to help. To the end of our lives most of us need that help – badly; and he wants to give it – very much.

… I like to reflect on Our Lord looking at me as I struggle to be what I know I should be, and fail; as I try to love both him and my neighbour, and get it wrong. But he knows that I want to try and that, surely, moves him to pity me.

To Be a Pilgrim, pp. 70, 72

In the Papal chapel there is a lovely crucifix made for Pope Paul VI when he was Archbishop of Milan. It has no crown of thorns and when the Pope remarked on this to the artist, he replied, 'No, the Lord has laid that on the head of the Archbishop of Milan.'

Light in the Lord, p. 133

*A*s a bishop ... you will be misunderstood, misrepresented, criticised, disliked and – the one that
hurts most – regarded as a disaster. I've had all those,
and I've learned thanks to them. It's a privilege to be
misunderstood, misrepresented, criticised, written off
as a disaster. It is a privilege, it is a grace, and I have
found nothing which has been more marvellous than
to realise that this cuts everything away from you
except the Lord ... It hurts, but it is a marvellous way
to grow in the Spirit.

UNPUBLISHED

I often think that if, as a bishop, I have just spent
the day saying 'thank you', and 'well done' to priests,
I have done a lot of my job because I believe that a lot
of our priests are discouraged and uncertain and need
our leadership and guidance, provided we can show a
degree of serenity and a degree of certainty.

LIGHT IN THE LORD, p. 143

I spend quite a lot of my life worrying because I am neglecting some part of my ministry. It is impossible to do adequately all that we are called to do, and I suspect that most bishops find that.

FOOTPRINTS OF THE NORTHERN SAINTS, p. 59

*W*e do most harm as bishops and priests when we are unkind.

FOOTPRINTS OF THE NORTHERN SAINTS, p. 59

*W*e must always be proud of the great martyr tradition. These were people who witnessed to the unity of the Church by their death, and you and I in our day must witness to the unity of the Church in our lives, remembering always that all denominations at the time of the Tudors and Stuarts had their martyrs. We must remember that great tradition, and we have to show the same zeal, the same devotion, the same courage as they.

UNPUBLISHED

I remember a remarkable man when I was a young monk. He had no education, no particular talents, but was a great man of prayer. He said to me: 'In the morning I go into church, and if I am not there God will want to know why I am not there.' He was clearly very close to God, but he could not tell you why or how and he could not have given a lecture on prayer. But he had learnt how to pray by just praying.

LIGHT IN THE LORD, pp. 119-20

*T*here is always the danger of a celibate becoming a bachelor in the wrong sense; to become self-regarding and surrounding himself with little comforts. Celibacy is not a choice of life by which we deny ourselves one thing, only to find compensation in others. The witness of celibacy must be something which is positive in itself and not in need of props and supports in order that it might be sustained.

LIGHT IN THE LORD, p. 40

Look back over the last month or so and see the number of occasions when, in small ways, you have been hurt; pin-pricks rather than a sword, and the number of times that has depressed you, understandably, and at the time it may have angered you …

A good practice, when you get that kind of situation, is to go down on your knees and say, 'Thank you, Lord.' In forty years of monastic life I achieved it once! But it worked so dramatically that I have never forgotten it. But I have never done it since, even though I still get upset by rude letters and all that kind of thing. I wish I could get into the habit of saying: 'Thank you, Lord, that in a very little way I have been allowed to share in your Passion.'

LIGHT IN THE LORD, pp. 131-2

There is no greater betrayal of another than to fail to love him or her.

SEARCHING FOR GOD, p. 238

*T*he art of schoolmastering can be summed up quite simply: it is to teach boys to teach themselves – to teach boys to teach themselves how to live, how to pray, how to work, how to direct their lives, how to shoulder responsibility and so forth. And we have to learn how much we can leave to the boys and how much we need to intervene to keep the balance. The balance implies knowing what is going on – how much we can leave to the boys and at what point we need to take the reins into our own hands; taking action in some cases and in others refraining from doing so ...

Little things can have a tremendous effect on boys. Years later a man of, say, twenty-five will meet you and say: 'I always remember the first thing you said to me. I arrived very nervous and worried about coming to school, and you said ...' You probably didn't say it, or you have forgotten, or it was something very trivial. But that is what one discovers in schoolmastering ... It is what we are that matters. It is the small things that count.

SEARCHING FOR GOD, pp. 116, 121-2

*A*s a schoolmaster I learned a very important truth. Looking after boys which was my task, I discovered that every boy between the ages of thirteen and eighteen (which was the age range in which I operated) was in some manner superior to me. He was something I could not be or he could do something which I couldn't do – even if it was only fixing a television set … The art of schoolmastering, the art of education, was to make that young person realise that he had a talent which I, as an adult, hadn't got. That was the basis of my respect for that person and also gave that person, that young life, a sense of his worth.

I could never be a teacher without being a learner – and leaders must always be learners.

UNPUBLISHED

*I*n our public life we move further and further away from God and the things of God, and yet in the hearts of men and women I believe that the yearning for God is becoming more and more intense.

TO BE A PILGRIM, p. 47

*I*n the 1950s, on a Sunday afternoon, there was a programme called *Top of the Pops*. At that time I was a housemaster, and my room would be crowded by the young who had to listen to it. I remember it vividly on one occasion when I had to prepare my lecture (I was teaching theology to younger monks), surrounded by forty youths listening to *Top of the Pops* – not the best situation for preparing a lecture on the existence of God! But on that day, I understood for the first time what I had been teaching in theology. It is a marvellous moment when suddenly you realise the things you have taught are true. It is a curious sensation; what Newman calls passing from notional to real assent.

UNPUBLISHED

*T*he Queen's Jubilee in 1977 proved to be a symbol of many values which had seemed in danger of eclipse. In the first place it stressed love of our country. That is not an outworn or irrelevant value. If we fail to love our country, what is there left to honour and revere? To love one's country is a virtue. Without honourable patriotism, how can one learn to give proper honour and respect to other countries and their peoples?

TO BE A PILGRIM, p. 178

I once met a high-powered businessman, who told me that he had trained himself always to act towards other people on the assumption that he liked them. If he had a difficult person to deal with, or if he had dealings with one he disliked, he would ask himself: 'What would I do if I really liked that person?' He then did it. Remarkable advice, and that way of handling people is entirely compatible with firmness. He was not only acting in a very Christ-like manner, but he ran an extraordinarily efficient and happy business on that basis.

To Be a Pilgrim, p. 112

*M*ary was sometimes puzzled and in distress. She had to flee with her son into Egypt; once she lost him on a pilgrimage. She saw him dying and in agony. It is sometimes like that for mothers. When it happens, it is hard to make sense of it. You have to trust and go on trusting.

To Be a Pilgrim, p. 204

Our Lady, on hearing that her cousin Elizabeth was going to become a mother, rushed over to visit her; which meant to look after her, care for her, be with her – it wasn't just popping over for an afternoon. Her cousin was advanced in years to have a child and Our Lady went over to share her joy and provide assistance. Her love was translated into action. Because it is what we *do* and not what we say that matters. What we do proves what we are, and Our Lady uprooted herself and went to help Elizabeth.

UNPUBLISHED

In my chapel I have a statue of Our Lady with her hands extended downwards. When I have insoluble problems to deal with I go to Our Lady, place my hands in hers and ask her to help me in my helplessness. I can then go back to my desk, confident that she has taken responsibility.

UNPUBLISHED

*I*n 1987 I visited St Thérèse's cell in the Carmel of Lisieux. By the door of her cell, scratched into the wood, she had written 'Jésus est mon unique amour' [Jesus is my only love]. That was not written in exaltation but in near despair. She was thus crying out to her beloved that even when she experienced nothing but absence, emptiness, darkness she clung to the assurance of being loved and carried in his arms. That is faith at a heroic level – that is trust, clinging to God when everything in our experience would seem to contradict his very existence or at least the fact of his love for us.

UNPUBLISHED

*I*t is a feminine trait to listen, to receive, to watch. Perhaps that is why more women pray than men. Perhaps that is why among contemplatives there are more women than men – it is the 'feminine' which listens and waits.

SEARCHING FOR GOD, p. 197

*A*nxious as we are to know what Our Lady looked like when she appeared at Lourdes, I find myself equally interested to know how Our Lady saw Bernadette. What did she see? She saw a girl about the same age as herself when the Angel Gabriel had appeared to her at the time of the Annunciation. She saw a girl like herself, neither famous nor well born – a girl who was poor.

Bernadette came from a family that could not have sunk any lower in terms of material prosperity and financial status. Nonetheless – and it is important to remember this – Bernadette possessed important qualities of character. She was quite strong-minded and completely honest. She had, too, the advantage of a supportive family and one which reacted with remarkable dignity to the pressures on its members.

LOURDES AND ITS VALUES, p. 9

*W*e are indeed clever, but not so wise. It is true wisdom which we need.

UNPUBLISHED

*I*f every single person is made in the image and likeness of God, then every single person can tell me something about God which nobody else can. ... That makes me very anxious to listen to everybody because they may be saying something that only they can say.

LIGHT IN THE LORD, p. 84

*M*any people need enemies for their own sense of identity. They are defined as much by what they oppose as by what they support. Conflict and confrontation characterise much of our politics, industrial relations and international affairs. Because of the way we have learned to think it is often easier to mobilise people to oppose than to co-operate. Hostility, anger and envy of others intensify. Those, however, who see themselves as children of God and as part of a single creation have to reject such attitudes and their destructive consequences. They develop partnership not conflict, friendship not hostility, peace not war.

UNPUBLISHED

*T*he real distinction is not between religion and life, but between what is real and what is illusory: between a life lived in the truth, and a life based on false hopes. Our faith reveals the truth about God and the truth about humanity, and so it is that St Irenaeus could say: 'The Glory of God is the human person fully alive.'

REMAKING EUROPE, p. 55

To Be a Pilgrim

*I go through life as a pilgrim, a pilgrim
who limps, which means that I go through
life as a wounded pilgrim. It is very important
to know one's woundedness and to accept it.
I don't think I have ever met a person who
was not in some way wounded, whether
by their background, their upbringing, early
disappointments, something that has happened
to them or something they have done.*

MYSTERY OF THE CROSS, p. 59

Quite often we simply do not know how to pray, and feel that deep sense of being lost. I think it is good at such times to see oneself rather like the lost sheep in the parable, caught in the briars, surrounded by fog, and the more you try to escape from the brambles the more you get entangled. The more you try to rush through the fog the more likely you are to get lost. When you are in that mood, wait and in your prayer imagine that sheep entangled in the briars with the fog all around. Just wait for him, Christ the Shepherd, to come through the fog and disentangle you …

In my life generally I feel empty in respect of the things of God. Paradoxically, it is all the negative things that bring us closer to God. When I am most empty, he is most able to fill me with his love, his ideas, his wishes, his will. So when you find yourself kneeling down in prayer, feeling totally empty, then a good tip is just to think of that poor old sheep caught in the briars, wandering around in the mist, totally lost.

LIGHT IN THE LORD, pp. 121, 124

I often tell the story of a chapel in Switzerland where I used to go and pray when I was a student, and there were lots of things written on the wall: 'Thank you for saving my life' – and one particular one: 'Thank you for *not* answering my prayer'. That is very profound. No prayer of asking is ever refused. You don't necessarily get the thing you ask for but you get the thing that draws you closer to God and *that's* what matters.

UNPUBLISHED

*N*o one prays easily at first, just as I think no one really enjoys the first glass of beer. You've got to get used to beer, then you get hooked on it and want more and more! Prayer is like that, you have got to get hooked but at the beginning it is hard going.

UNPUBLISHED

*P*rayer is to the life of the spirit what breathing is to the life of the body.

TO BE A PILGRIM, p. 133

*I*f you bring prayer into your life, and if you stay at it, there are moments when you just know that God is present. You don't see him, you're not talking, but somehow you just know he is present, and that is a moment to relish and it is a gift – a gift that is given if you decide to make prayer part of your life, and if you keep trying, day in and day out, sometimes fighting the doubts of your faith, sometimes feeling totally inadequate, perhaps feeling you have wandered too far away. But stick at it, and then there comes that moment of peace which is gift from God.

UNPUBLISHED

*T*he only 'failure' in prayer is when we neglect it. The only 'success' in prayer is the sense of God's presence, or a deep peace and sense of well-being, a marvellous moment of inner freedom. When that comes, it is a special gift from God. We have no claim on it, we cannot demand it. Our part is to turn to him as best we can, trying to raise our minds and hearts to him.

MYSTERY OF LOVE, p. 30

God is bad on the telephone. I will give an example. My aunt Betty could not come to terms with modern life so could not cope at all with the telephone. If you rang her up she more or less panicked and just didn't know what to say. So when I rang her up she never said anything and I just chatted away, but I knew she was pleased to hear from me, and I was just glad to know she was at the other end of the telephone for I was very fond of her and had every reason to believe she was fond of me. That is what prayer is like for most of us. We feel we are chatting away and getting no answer, but somehow we know that God is at the other end.

UNPUBLISHED

The way into Wonderland is through Blunderland. God can get you in the quick way round the edges, but that is not usual. So Blunderland is the spiritual life, the school where you learn about God. Wonderland is heaven, where we see God. And through the dark glass all around, you get some little glimpses of God when you're in Blunderland.

UNPUBLISHED

*M*ost of us live in a muddle, full of uncertainties and hesitations, with confused ideas about God, often haunted by feelings of guilt. Words addressed to God and thoughts about him mean little or nothing. God allows the experience in order to free us from the wrong attachments and draw us to himself. It is good to feel futile before God and wait patiently for him to find us. We may be deprived of the joy of sensing his presence, but we give to him the joy of our trusting him, especially when that trust is given in the dark and without seeking reward. Love of God grows when faith is purified.

Mystery of Love, p. 27

*O*urs may well be an age of outstanding discovery and achievement, but it is also an age of deep confusion.

Unpublished

*N*o way of life, no set of responsibilities excludes people from sanctity, nor dispenses them from striving for it.

To Be a Pilgrim, p. 203

*D*o not despair
nor give up hope.
However far
you may have wandered,
whatever wrong
you may have done,
despair must never be
a word for you.
He wants us,
wants us more
than we have
ever wanted him,
or ever could.

UNPUBLISHED

*M*any people simply have not got the time or the energy to do much more than get through the day, and care for their families and their own homes. But I would think that most of us could find close at hand an old or a sick person whom we can visit once in a while.

TO BE A PILGRIM, p. 113

*P*eople on a journey of faith need each other.

UNPUBLISHED

*I*n Ethiopia, during the famine of 1984, I was in a camp where people were waiting for food that would never come, and a nun called Sister Gabriel tugged my sleeve saying: 'Come and see my special friends.' She was in her late eighties and had been in prison in China for twenty years. Those special friends were in an old shack, and were the ones least likely to be fed for they had lost limbs, and were mad. But she ministered to them, and as I watched her walking round I saw in a remarkable way the face of Christ in that woman.

When we serve others in great generosity we become like Christ. Doctors, nurses, and many others – they become like Christ. He leaves his image in them.

UNPUBLISHED

$\mathcal{A}$s I was passing a row of people [in Ethiopia] I looked into the eyes of an old, old man sitting next to his wife. They were in the last hours of their lives. Somehow or other he must have sensed that I was a priest. I knew he was a Christian because he had, as Coptic Christians do, a cross marked on his forehead. As I looked into his eyes I thought, in a strange way, that he had compassion on me. Here was I, a well-fed cleric, living in an affluent part of Europe, with a roof over my head. But he had a marvellous serenity and a wonderful freedom, and I came away asking myself which of the two of us was the more to be pitied?

UNPUBLISHED

$\mathcal{A}$s I got out of the helicopter in the Ethiopian camp, a small boy aged about ten came straight up to me and took hold of my hand. He was dressed only in a loin-cloth around his waist, and was of course looking very hungry. As he took my hand, with the other one he pointed to his mouth to indicate his hunger.

I said to the interpreter: 'Tell him I've come so that I can go home and make certain that food will be sent to him by our people, and that I've got no food in my pocket.' He went on making this gesture and then a strange thing happened, because he alternated that gesture by taking my hand and rubbing it against his cheek …

This child, who could not speak my language and I could not speak his, was yet able to communicate his need for food and his need for love, by those two gestures – pointing to his mouth with one hand and with the other rubbing my hand against his cheek. I saw in that child the fundamental, basic needs of every human: the need for *life*, for it is food and drink that give life, and the need for *love*. We crave to live and we crave to love and be loved.

When the time came for me to go and I got into the helicopter, this child stood and looked at me very reproachfully; there was a kind of look in his eyes: 'Why are you leaving me behind?' It has haunted me ever since because I wonder what happened to that child.

UNPUBLISHED

*P*ower, possessions and pleasure can be false gods. Used rightly they are good things; used wrongly they can, and do, wreak havoc in our lives.

TO BE A PILGRIM, p. 160

Our family lived at No. 4. We were three girls and two boys. Up the street there lived at No. 11 three unmarried ladies and their brother. I was in love with one of the ladies. But there was quite a problem because of an age discrepancy. I was aged four, pushing five, and she was seventy-two, possibly seventy-three. About once a year we were invited to No. 11 for tea. On arrival we were each given the end of a coloured cotton. We each had our own colour. We then proceeded to follow the cotton up the stairs, in and out of bedrooms until finally we arrived at the present destined for each one of us.

Then one day the brother died and his sisters mourned him, and so did we. His name was Frank. Why had he died? Where had he gone? Encounter with death at an early age makes the young ask grown-up questions. We did. And the sisters? They were sad, very sad. If only … if only … why him? Why now? Such thoughts, and the sadness, that is their companion, is part of every family's story.

UNPUBLISHED

*I*n practice we have to learn to be compassionate
when we are young. It doesn't start in the Third
World, it doesn't start in the parish, it starts in the
home. That is where you learn to be compassionate –
learning to say 'no' to my inevitable tendency to be
self-centred and learning to be generous to others. It is
checking myself when I am impatient, especially with
my parents, when I am intolerant with other people
or quick to be judgmental. I have to learn young
to be concerned for the old, concerned for the sick,
concerned for the handicapped, concerned for the
poor, for the marginal. They are not 'over there' but
probably next door or in the home.

UNPUBLISHED

*T*here is a difference between just 'saying' prayers and
'praying' prayers. When you say a prayer try to think
either about the words you are reading or reciting,
or about the person to whom you are addressing the
words. That sounds elementary enough, but it is surprising how difficult it is to do.

TO BE A PILGRIM, p. 127

When I was very young I was told about a small boy who went into a larder and seeing a large pile of apples wanted to take one. He knew he shouldn't without asking, but everyone was out, and as there were so many apples nobody would know if there was one short. That story ate into my soul because it was pointed out to me that although nobody would know, one person would and that was God. So for years after I thought of God as someone watching me all the time to see if I was getting it right, and catching me out if I got it wrong.

It took me forty years to recover from that story! Years later I discovered God was the sort of person who would nudge me and say 'take two'! I've told this story before and had letters saying: 'Dear Cardinal, don't you think it's very wicked to teach the young that God wants them to steal apples?'

UNPUBLISHED

What is appealing about rogues – not the wicked or evil person – is their humility. You never meet a conceited rogue!

MYSTERY OF LOVE, p. 23

*I*t is exhilarating to discover another who will captivate our heart and occupy the empty space within it. It is thrilling to realise that we have a privileged place in someone else's heart and life. There is no need to elaborate on that experience. We discover that love can raise us to the heights, and also plunge us to the depths of despair. We find that human love can be fickle. But in my teens I began to learn that in some way we are made for love, and that all true human love, however transient and imperfect, has in it something of the infinite and eternal.

UNPUBLISHED

*H*ope is a Christian virtue and it is as important as faith and charity. This is not said often enough. People probably hear many sermons on faith and love, but not many on hope. Rarely do we see an article on hope, or see commended to us the importance of being cheerful and happy, in spite of the trials of life, in spite of the difficulties we meet. A true Christian would perhaps say '*because* of the trials, *because* of the difficulties'.

TO BE A PILGRIM, p. 121

*P*ilgrims are on their way to some place; there is a destination. I would find it very hard to accept that after life on this earth there is no more 'me', and nothing for me; no more 'you', and nothing for you. It would not make sense of life, and no sense of death.

UNPUBLISHED

*W*e can no longer remain indifferent when those who are one with us in Jesus Christ suffer injustice, exploitation and discrimination. We are called to act and to suffer, if necessary, on their behalf.

UNPUBLISHED

'*P*rayer is the raising of the mind and heart to God.' In my view, there is no better definition of prayer than that given in the Catechism. That definition did not say 'raised' but 'raising' the mind and heart, attempting to lift them up to God. For prayer consists in *trying* to get my mind up to God and *trying* to get my heart involved with God. The operative word is 'trying'.

LIGHT IN THE LORD, p. 118

*T*he 'prayer of incompetence': most of us know this type of prayer all too well. It occurs when thoughts about God or anything spiritual are quite impossible, and when our desiring is confused and unclear. This kind of thing can happen when we are anxious and worried, full of cares at work or in the home, or perhaps when we are simply 'out of sorts' or unwell. We have no taste for prayer. It would be much easier to omit it altogether. When that is the mood, then we have to make a deliberate decision to pray. Set time aside, survive through all the difficulties, but stay there, just to show God that we want to please him. There is great merit in that prayer, even if we don't get much in terms of joy and immediate reward.

To Be a Pilgrim, p. 129

*I*f you have distractions, then turn your distractions into your prayer. (If a car passes the window in the wrong gear, then say something to God about the driver – I mean a kind prayer for the welfare of the driver, not necessarily about his driving or gear box!)

To Be a Pilgrim, p. 137

I know that, for my part, I need to make space each morning for half an hour of prayer. Experience has also taught me that when mental prayer seems to be quite hopeless (when distracted, suffering from dryness, upset, tired, with no taste for the task) then reading, either from the Bible or from some spiritual book, can transform the quality of prayer. It may not be easy to find space for that half hour (especially once the work of the day has begun); it is very much harder to make time for spiritual reading. It is the first element of prayer to be squeezed out of the day's routine, and it is a loss.

LIGHT IN THE LORD, p. 114

*M*ost of us when we pray find that our minds are full of very ordinary things, maybe something we have done or are about to do, or the problems everybody has throughout life. These are often called 'distractions' and the only way to cope with them is to make them part of your prayer. If God became man – which indeed he did – then that made holy all things human, and everything human, except sin, is pleasing to God.

LIGHT IN THE LORD, p. 120

$\mathcal{P}$lan to pray; do not leave it to chance. Select a time and a place (a room at home, on the bus, taking a walk).

Decide on how long you will spend in trying to pray (five minutes, ten, fifteen, thirty or more).

Decide what you are going to do when you pray – e.g. which prayer to select to say slowly and lovingly; or which passage from the Bible to read prayerfully. Sometimes use your own words; sometimes just be still and silent. Follow your inclination.

Always start by asking the Holy Spirit for help in your prayers. Pray: 'Come Holy Spirit, teach me to pray; help me to do it.'

Remember you are trying to get in touch with a Person, and that Person is God – Father or Son or Holy Spirit. He is wanting to get in touch with you.

Don't be a slave to one way of praying. Choose the one you find easiest, and try some other method when the one you are using becomes a burden or doesn't help.

Don't look for results.

If you always feel dry and uninterested at prayer, then read a spiritual book or pamphlet. An article in a Catholic paper may be a help. Spiritual reading is important.

Trying to pray *is* praying. Never give up trying.

To Be a Pilgrim, p. 137

Quite often I go to pray and find it difficult to concentrate on God. In my head there is a succession of thoughts and images, and most are quite irreligious. It occurred to me that I should invite God to come and sit by my side. Then I would say to him, 'All these thoughts and images which are rushing through my mind, I ask you to watch them with me.' And so these images and thoughts become my prayer because I have asked him to watch them with me. It doesn't always make coping with distractions any easier. I just try to say a quick word to God: 'Help me to bring you into my confused thoughts.' So I reflect: that tricky problem I must face tomorrow, or next Saturday's football results (I sometimes score a really good goal – I am ashamed about that, I mean about the distraction, not the goal – it was quite brilliant!), or the birthday present I have forgotten to buy. 'Bring them to God,' I say to myself. If I learn to take my distractions to God, then I get into the habit of bringing God into my daily life.

BASIL IN BLUNDERLAND, p. 32

DEATH AND ETERNITY

*Judgment is whispering into
the ear of a merciful and
compassionate God the story
of my life I have never been
able to tell anyone.*

UNPUBLISHED

*T*here is no tidy, rational explanation of the crushing burden of suffering. We cannot work out easy answers about why it should be. God gave us instead not an answer, but a way to find the answer. It is the cross that will reveal it, but it has be a personal discovery. You cannot begin to see pattern and purpose unless you have known the cross and blindly let Jesus lead you from despair into hope.

To BE A PILGRIM, p. 220

*T*rying to pray *is* praying. Our part is to go on trying. Stairs have a lesson to teach, putting our foot on that first step, painfully, doggedly. Then from time to time the Father will come down, pick us up and carry us to the top. In God's way of doing things, if he ever does carry us to the top, he then always puts us back again at the bottom of the stairs to start all over again. It is only right at the end of life that he takes us to the top and keeps us there.

To BE A PILGRIM, pp. 137-8

*E*amonn Andrews[7] in his most famous television series [*This Is Your Life*] depended much on the element of surprise. I like to think that even now he has experienced the most astounding surprise of all, or is at least on the way to it. I trust that he has been able to see the meaning of Scripture, 'Eye hath not seen, nor ear heard, neither hath it entered into the heart of man what things God hath prepared for them that love him' (1 Cor. 2:9).

UNPUBLISHED

*D*eath is neither a disaster nor a defeat but leads us into the fullness of life with God. That life is union with him, love's greatest experience. We are made for that. We take comfort from the conviction that in life or in death we are at all times in the hands of a God who loves and whom we are to call Father. No torment can touch us if our lives are upright, faithful and compassionate.

UNPUBLISHED

I have discovered in my life that I have never really met anybody who could understand me as I wish to be understood, who would give me that kind of forgiveness which deep down I feel I want, who could give me that total healing, and console me in need. The person who will understand, who will heal, forgive and console – that is my view of God.

UNPUBLISHED

*I*f we kiss the crucifix, we shall discover him who suffered like us and for us. That kissing can, sometimes, more easily be done, when words seem empty and meaningless. It is a way of saying 'Into thy hands I commend my spirit' and often it is the best way, perhaps the only way. Relief from pain and sorrow may not be immediate; indeed we may be called to walk further carrying our cross, but the yoke will be sweeter and the burden lighter. Of course we cannot, and must not, rejoice in the pain. That would be to do violence to our instincts and to our natures. We are not made for pain; we are made for happiness. But in recoiling from the cross, as is natural, we can yet rejoice in the carrying of it, but it must be for his sake. He in us and we in him.

TO BE A PILGRIM, pp. 97-8

*T*here is, to my way of thinking at any rate, no adequate explanation of why there should be suffering in a world made and loved by God. I am baffled by it, and I am sure that you must be as well. The only explanation that makes sense comes, I would suggest, from looking at the image of Christ dying on the cross, and knowing that the figure of the crucifix was not overcome by death. When the hopes and expectations of his friends seemed to be buried with him in the tomb, new hope sprang forth from the midst of despair when he rose from the dead. He made all things new, suffering and death as well, your suffering and your death too.

To Be a Pilgrim, p. 98

*A*fter death, we shall be pure contemplatives looking at God who is truth, who is all goodness, and who is all beauty.

UNPUBLISHED

*D*o not be fearful of death. Welcome it when it comes, It is now a holy thing, made so by him who died that we might live.

To Be a Pilgrim, p. 228

$\mathcal{A}$t some time in our lives, we may feel that we are failures. We have experienced great disappointments, and the sense of being less good than we should be, of being less successful than we would like to be. This sense of failure and inadequacy is common among us. Our Lord must have felt like this at the end of his life. Everybody had turned against him. They were going to execute him; they were insulting him. We know that this moment of failure was God's moment of success ... Whenever I feel inadequate or a failure, disappointed or upset, God can enter into my life, and bring his success.

TO BE A PILGRIM, p. 68

$\mathcal{W}$hen we were very young, surely we often went to sleep with somebody telling us a story. I like to think that God whispers stories into our ears as we go to sleep. Perhaps the story he whispers into your ear tonight is: I have something good for you later on.

UNPUBLISHED

Some years ago in Frascati in Italy, a small child, three or four years of age, fell into a mine shaft and became trapped halfway down. Rescuers worked day and night to reach the child whose helpless crying could be heard by all those who waited nearby. As the rescuers worked on, the child's mother kept vigil at the top of the shaft, anguished and distraught. The crying grew weaker as the child's life ebbed away. The world waited. The child died.

With the death of that child something nearly died in me – my trust in God's love and goodness ...

There are no quick answers. The mystery of God is too great, and our minds too small, too limited to understand his ways. But I cannot, and will not doubt the love of God for every person, a love that is warm, intimate and true. I shall trust him, even when I find no human grounds for doing so ...

If you have known utter desolation, so has Christ. And what was going through his mother's mind as she kept vigil by the cross, anguished and distraught? She shared her Son's agony as only a mother can. She watched. She waited. And Jesus died. It is hard for anyone who is not a mother to understand a mother's anguish when her child is dying.

MYSTERY OF THE CROSS, pp. 9, 10

*F*irst thoughts about death are normally ones of fear and dread. It is partly having to face the unknown, partly the recoiling from the final agony, as we lie helpless and perhaps wired up to all those machines competing for access to our body. On a bad day there is that common fear which tells us that there is no future, only a blank, nothing. We are no more. And then another thought comes to trouble us and it is how quickly we are forgotten …

Then in a very bad moment I think about the relief my demise will bring to some people. I do worry about the insensitive and clumsy ways I have handled some people, about my selfishness … No I won't go on listing my faults here. 'Don't forget,' I once heard a great abbot say, 'when you are dead somebody will be relieved' …

BASIL IN BLUNDERLAND, pp. 72-3

*T*he meaning of things, and their purpose,
is in part now hidden
but shall in the end become clear.
The choice is between
the Mystery and the absurd.
To embrace the Mystery
is to discover the real.
It is to walk towards the light,
to glimpse the morning star, to catch sight
from time to time
of what is truly real.
It is no more than a flicker of light
through the cloud of unknowing,
a fitful ray of light
that is a messenger from the sun
which is hidden from your gaze.
You see the light but not the sun.
When you set yourself to look more closely,
you will begin to see some sense
in the darkness that surrounds you.
Your eyes will begin to pick out
the shape of things and persons around you.

You will begin to see in them
the presence of the One
who gives them meaning and purpose
and that it is he
who is the explanation of them all.

MYSTERY OF THE INCARNATION, p. v

*W*ho remembers a common thief,
dying on a cross
for the wrong
he has done?
Who will stand by him
claim his friendship?
That thief prays
'Remember me when thou comest
into thy kingdom – '

The answer comes:

'This day thou wilt be with me
in paradise.'

UNPUBLISHED

$\mathcal{W}$e are left to continue our pilgrimage through life, weep and mourn.[8] Sadness reigns in our hearts. You, Diana, and your companions too, are on your way to union with him who loves you so. He knows the love which you, Diana, had for others. God speaks now of his love for you. Our tears will not be bitter ones now but a gentle weeping to rob our sadness of its agony and lead at last to peace, peace with God.

MYSTERY OF THE CROSS, p. 73

$\mathcal{G}$rief cannot be shared, for it is mine alone.
Grief is a dying within me,
a great emptiness,
a frightening void.
It is loneliness,
a sickening sorrow at night,
on awakening a terrible dread.
Another's words do not help.
A reasoned argument explains little
for having tried too much.
Silence is the best response to another's grief.
Not the silence that is a pause in speech,
awkward and unwanted,
but one that unites heart to heart.

Love, speaking in silence, is the way into
the void of another's grief.
The best of all loves comes silently,
and slowly too, to soften the pain of grief,
and begin to dispel the sadness.
It is the love of God, warm and true,
which will touch the grieving heart and heal it.

He looks at the grieving person and has pity,
for grief is a great pain.
He came among us to learn about grief,
and much else too, this Man of Sorrows.
He knows. He understands.
Grief will yield to peace – in time.

UNPUBLISHED

*H*ave you felt abandoned?
and abandoned by God too?
So did he.

UNPUBLISHED

I see this life as a period of training, a time of
preparation, during which we learn the art of loving
God and our neighbour, which is the heart of the
gospel message. Sometimes succeeding, sometimes
failing. As we learn, then many things begin to look
different. Death, for instance, comes to be seen as the
way which leads us to the vision of God, the moment
when we shall see him as he really is, and find our total
fulfilment in love's final choice. The ultimate union
with that which is most lovable, union with God. I
call that the moment of ecstasy.

MYSTERY OF LOVE, p. 54

'*I*nto your hands
I commend my spirit.'
That was the password
into his presence,
into those hands,
safe hands,
stretching out
to receive
his weary soul.

UNPUBLISHED

Notes

1 *Ampleforth Journal* (Summer 1976).
2 *Midrash Rabba I, Genesis Rabba*, Commentary by Bernard Marauni, *Bereshit V* (Paris, 1987), quoted by Christian Duquoc in *Concilium* (August 1992), p. 9.
3 *Rule of St Benedict*, Prologue.
4 Sermon at Ampleforth following the announcement of his elevation to the See of Westminster.
5 Benedictine Vespers in Westminster Abbey following his installation as Archbishop in Westminster Cathedral, 25 March 1976.
6 Barnabas Sandeman OSB, writing in the *Ampleforth Journal* (Spring 1979).
7 Memorial Mass for Eamonn Andrews, 7 December 1987.
8 On the death of Diana, Princess of Wales, 1997.